PRACTICAL
Philosophy of TAO
for teachers and individuals

SIMPLIFIED AND ILLUSTRATED

by
Myke Symonds

Life Force publishing, UK.

ISBN (13) 978-0-9542932-0-8
ISBN (10) 0-9542932-0-7
EAN 9780954293208

16 point main body Text for easy reading.

Life Force Publishing (UK)™©
Life Force Books©

You may find other books by the same author by searching for "books by Mike Symonds" (using the common or expected spelling).

Preface

This book has been produced as a response to the lack of factual information regarding Tao and Taoism and the graphical representations used in this world-wide philosophy. For many years Tao has been misrepresented, translations confused (sometimes deliberately by religious drum-beaters) and generally overlooked by the greater public because of translations which can barely be understood.

Taoism is a simple philosophy, not a religion. In its pure form it uses simple yet amazing symbols or graphics which can be easily understood when explained, even by those who cannot read: and there were plenty around who could not read between 2,000 and 5,000 years ago.

Schools especially will benefit from this book in Religious Studies or R.E., as it will not only serve to give young people a sense of China's most important philosophical background but a "common sense" philosophy which can be directly applied to living in today's society. As well as providing much needed moral guidelines, so lacking these days, but if studied it is plain to see that the many great Taoist adepts were also responsible for discovering many inventions and scientific facts, like the so-called "Big Bang" theory, written by Taoist over 2,000 years ago! As we in the West and East "progress" (a doubtful concept!) so it is being discovered that more and more of the Taoist concepts and writings become more and more accurate, acceptable and relevant; making this wonderfully deep philosophy something which should be included in modern educational establishments.

☼ Teacher: You will find these "bright idea" symbols throughout the book where teachers can gain instant ideas for stimulative conversation, homework studies or essays on thoughts.

DEDICATION
To My Old Friend
Tim Denyer
Chinese Arts Practitioner
A good friend and father to Lilly
Died prematurely through a blood clot at age 60

¤

Acknowledgements

Respects to all "Tao scientists" past and present.

My friends and colleagues in the Arts who have all in their own way made this possible.

My Taoist Arts Master, Prof. Soo, Clifford Chee. For his insight, energies and enlightened teachings.

My students who constantly ask questions, keeping me on my toes, and listen to long answers with patience!

Special thanks to Zoe Simpson for her editorial work and encouragement.

¤

Contents

道 TAO (pronounced "Dow")

Chinese does not translate accurately into English as the calligraphy is 'pictograph': it is a graphic symbol or image of a word, name or meaning. The nearest translation of TAO is 'WAY', however this can change according to the context of the sentence it is put into, so therefore could mean 'Path', but the literal translation from traditional Mandarin Chinese is 'Way' or 'Truth' but can also mean 'Path' as the two ancient pictographs it is made up from represent 'head' and 'walk' which may be translated as "journey of consciousness". Chinese calligraphy, pre-modern Simplified, can mean different things according to the context of the sentence or surrounding characters.

What does this mean?

Tao or Way refers to the Universe. The Universe is too big to imagine or know fully, but being in one tiny part of it on our World (Earth) we can see the actions of the Way all around us. This we call 'Nature' and also 'Natural Phenomenon'. Tao is everything in the Universe, all substance, all matter and anti-matter, all planets, life and even dust. Tao is everything and the way that existence happens, creation, birth, life, death, interaction and even non-action (stillness).

Sometimes the Chinese will refer to Tao as "T'ai Chi" (pron. "Tie-chee"), meaning Supreme Ultimate[1]. This is because nothing can be greater than Tao, nothing can change it, nothing can interfere with it as it will always override any

1

This is not the same as T'ai Chi Ch'uan, or Taijiquan, the Martial Art, as "Ch'uan" means Fist or Exercise (we would say Boxing perhaps), in this case T'ai Chi Ch'uan means "Self-defence Exercise Form which follows the principles of the Supreme Ultimate or Tao".

attempt to change the true course of nature: example – this is like an old building which has been left unattended, soon it will start to decay, fall apart and be grown over by plants, worn down by the weather and eventually leave little trace. Nature is supreme and cannot be changed or tampered with.

Tao is the Ultimate Reality. The supreme being is beyond words, we only use the word Tao to let others know what we are talking about, otherwise it is nameless, shapeless, beyond description and understanding. We, as humans, can see and feel the *effects* of Tao. The name "Tao" has been used to describe the entire workings of the Universe, various other names are used to describe parts of Tao, like Yin and Yang, the two main forces or actions.

What is Taoism? 蘯

Taoism (pron. as "Dow-izm") is the practice of following Tao or trying to understand it. It is a Philosophy, not a religion. A Philosophy is something which may be a Humanistic Belief, a School of Thought or a Practice. Taoism is many things to many people. Christianity was started by the followers of Christ (not Christ, he was not a Christian but a Jew) just over 2,000 years ago. Taoism was started by philosophers over 5,000 years ago and has developed ever since. Many Taoists are constantly engaged in services to humanity, discovering more about the way we live, healthier diets, healing, balanced exercises and practises that help people grow stronger and live healthier lives, cosmology and so on.

A person wishing to understand Tao may observe Nature, take part in exercises which follow Taoist principles, like Taijiquan (pronounced "Tie-chee-chew-aan") and even meditations. The written guidelines are studied and the relationship between Tao and the person's life are studied and evaluated. As impossible as it may seem to develop mentally from a physical exercise, or so it seems at first, Arts like T'ai Chi Ch'uan do have a very profound effect on not only the body, but the Mind and the Psyche too. A good teacher will be able to spot where you are "imbalanced" by the way you move or stand, so transforming the physical, which then has an effect on the relationship between body, energy and Mind. Hence there is a saying in Taoist Arts that they practice "alchemy", thus transforming "lead into gold".

Look at the author's posture in this movement from Taiji Dao (a more advanced form of Taijiquan that is learned after Open Hand and Staff 'Kun' Forms.) See the symmetry of posture? Note the "opening" of the body, with twisting: all these varied movement aid far better health through transformations within.

Is it a Religion?

A Religion is a belief, a Theological Virtue or system of Faith, usually *followed* rather than *participated* in like Taoism. A Taoist "adept" is a person who seeks to live by Tao and seek harmony. Famous philosopher and psychologist, Dr. Carl Gustav Jung, studied many major religions and found that they all had virtually the same aims, morals and essence at their core and that the differences were caused only by culture, society trends and humanistic interpretation, etcetera. He reasoned that all religions were the result of accrued wisdom by study: nature, universal principles, etcetera. Dr. Jung became Taoist in his approach and used the ("Ye-jing") I-Ching or "Book of Changes" when he struggled to find answers in his personal life.

Harmony.

Because Tao represents nature, a more natural lifestyle may be followed by the person or student of the Way. These might include wearing natural fibres, not man-made, becoming vegetarian, studying Taoist works and history and any branch of Taoist Arts: Taijiquan, Qigong ("Chee-gong") for Health, Meditations, Feng Shui ("Fung Shu-ay"), Acupressure and Taoist Healing, Balancing Ch'ang Ming "Long Life" Diet (See book T'ai Chi Diet II - Ch'ang Ming - ISBN-9780954293239) and/or other practices which use Taoist Principles.

☼ What is "Harmony" and why or where is it needed?

It is widely known that becoming a Vegetarian can reduce toxins and harmful chemicals within the body, prolong life, help towards a clearer mind and better life, avoiding many illnesses such as Cancer and common diseases. The Human vegetable chewing teeth and long intestines. Someone who wishes to reach the highest levels of understanding might go so far as to live a life away from most others, spending much time in meditation and honing reasoning processes: typical of the "monks" of Wudang in China, living in caves and monasteries atop the Wudang Mountains.

Trying to avoid things which are not natural is a typical practice for a Taoist. This can be very hard in modern culture, especially in cities or industrialised areas where natural food, natural clothing and natural living habitat are almost impossible to come by, let alone distractions from unnecessary paraphernalia.

With food, try to avoid animal flesh (meat), anything which is "processed", too much Yang (like salt) or too much Yin (like sugar), out of season fruits and vegetables, acidic tropical fruit or spices when the weather is cold or damp, and excess of foods – imbalance – and foods which contain poisons or toxins, like green potatoes, rhubarb and spinach. (I alert you to my book T'ai Chi Diet: food for life' which is based on the Taoist C'hang-ming and explains what foods are, what they do and how they may heal or harm.)

With clothing you should try to avoid unnatural or man-made fibres, like Nylon, as this can upset the body's natural energies (Ch'i/Qi) and can be seen to attract one of the elements of Ch'i, Static Electricity, which is produced in the body and flows through the Meridians or Energy Channels – as treated in Acupuncture.

In living or working conditions as natural as possible climate should be developed. Much illness is thought to be caused by unnaturally produced energy fields, such as electrical Ring Mains, computers, radio and telephone signals: there is a disturbing trend for headphones (magnetic field), all "Wireless", mobile phones and other gadgets, which we really could live without[2]. Often we only hear about the most obvious cases, for example, where someone living almost underneath high voltage pylons and power cables becomes ill with Leukaemia, linking it with other similar cases. Household, office and school wiring could be shielded, if given enough thought and care, so people's health improved and risk of induced illness decreased.

The Three Treasures.

The 'Three Jewels' improve the quality of life. A Taoist will try to live by these codes of conduct. They are:

1. Compassion, kindness and gentleness. These can be translated many ways, but generally imply being good to others, not harming anyone and caring for others.

2. Frugality, charity and moderation. Mostly these speak for themselves. Being kind, giving without thought of reward, being "sparing" yet giving just enough, moderation in all things and not being excessive.

3. Not daring to be first in the world. Ego, often the downfall of many a human, is something to be kept under control. Do not desire to be first, but strive to complete your life in the best way possible.

---

2 Modern science has discovered that the main sources of Ch'i or Qi in our body can be named as Low Frequency Modulation Infra-red Microwaves, Static electricity and Electro-magnetic Energy. These work within their own natural system and create natural energy fields. If these energy fields are disturbed or destroyed then health can be damaged, if not corrected the situation, a pathogen, gets worse and serious illness or death can follow. To understand more about Ch'i the author directs you towards his book 'Qigong & Baduanjin' – paperback.

Together, 'The Three Treasures', they make for better morals and less aggravation within society.

How does this deal with the perceived need to compete, to be better than others in order to make a living? The answer to that is inside yourself. The "ideal" in Taoism is not to compete, but to make yourself as good as you possibly can be. If you do that, in your chosen career or way of life, then there is no need to compete. By being as good as you can be, you will be a great person to deal with, and offer a really efficient and friendly service, with a conscientious eye to detail. That will set you apart from those who set-up a false image just to make money!

Buddhism, which has become really popular in recent years, has "borrowed" these elements from Taoism. However, Buddha was not a Buddhist, and never intended his teachings to do anything rather than enlighten people as to "better ways". Taoism is not a religion, regardless of how some may treat it. Taoism, although having a network of friends, colleagues and schools of activity, is just a method for self-development. Therefore you should never hear of anyone using Taoism to start a war or do things which are inhuman or unjust. Taoism, which has a liberal collection of Confucian morals and family values believes in the famous old saying:

"Do as you would be done by."

Taoist Philosophy

The philosophy of Tao was written many years ago and created by many thousands, if not millions, of Taoists. Perhaps the most notable are Lao Tzu and Huang Ti. Huang-Ti ("Huang-di") - The Yellow Emperor.

Huang-di, the Yellow Emperor, is a legendary Chinese sovereign and a popular cultural hero who is considered in Chinese mythology to be the ancestor of all the Han Chinese. Huang-di reigned from 2497 BCE to 2398 BCE. His personal or family given name was said to be Gōngsūn Xuānyuán. Huang-di was hailed as a chief deity of Taoism during the Han Dynasty (202 BCE-220 CE)[3].

Huang-di became very interested in Tao and its principles. He gathered as much information from across China as he could; an incredible task, considering there was no postal service, radio or television and very few books in those times. The Emperor selected Five Personal Advisers (three woman and two men) who were responsible for collecting or evaluating facts. They looked into every aspect of life, from diet and health to marriage and relationships, to living and dying.

Among many accomplishments, Huang-di has been accredited with "The Yellow Emperor's Canon of Internal Medicine". The Huang-di Neijing, said to be authored in collaboration with his physician Qibo ("Chee-bo"); some modern historians think it was compiled from ancient sources by a scholar living between the Zhou and Han dynasties, more than 2,000 years later and some now believe

---

3

Not to be confused with Shih Huang Di, the later "despotic" ruler and distinctly non-Taoist.

that Qibo was in fact Hippocrates (*ca.* 460 BC – *ca.* 370 BC): believed to be the author of the Hippocratic Oath, which Doctors swear by to this day.

Huang-di's interest in natural health and preventing and treating diseases, according to historical sources, meant he lived to the age of 100, and attained immortality after his physical death. Huang-di is an important figure in Chinese religions, particularly Taoism and Confucianism. He introduced the earliest form of formalised Martial Arts into China, because he was also good in medicine, he knew that Martial Art was beneficial for both good health and self-defence.

Huang-di is said to have ruled for 100 years, had 25 children, 14 of whom were sons. Of these 14 sons, 12 chose last names for themselves. It is also said that all the noble families of the first 3 dynasties of China, Xia, Shang and Zhou were all direct descendants of Huang-di. The Korean descendant of Huang-di include the family Paik of Suwon region in Korea (other possible transliteration: Baik, Back, Paek, Beak, Paek, Baek) and the first figure to arise as a self-identified Korean is Woo-Kyung Paik.

When Huang-di had lived for over 100 years, he arranged his worldly affairs with his ministers, and prepared for his journey to the Heavens. One version said a Dragon came down from the Heaven and took Huang-di away. Another version said Huang-di himself turned into half-man and half Dragon and flew away.

Huang-di, through his study and help of his Five Personal Advisers who collated information from all over China, is accredited with laying the first organised foundations of Taoist belief. He also commissioned and possibly even took part in the design of many inventions. Overall he was a highly intelligent man and remains a worthy and highly respected icon of Chinese history; and should really be included in world-wide schools history lessons[4].

4   Especially as the Chinese invented most things that we take for granted today.

The Old Master

Lao-zi (Chinese: pinyin: Lǎozǐ; Wade-Giles: Laosi; also Lao Tse, Lao-Tzu, Laotze and other variations) was a philosopher of ancient China and is a central figure in Taoism ("Daoism"). Lao-zi literally means "Old Master" and is generally considered an honorific or respectful title. Laozi is revered as a god in religious forms of Taoism. Taishang Laojun is a title for Laozi in the Taoist religion, which refers to him as "One of the Three Pure Ones".

According to Chinese tradition, Laozi lived in the 6th century BC. Historians variously contend facts simply because many old records have been lost or destroyed and they have to make guesses. The fact remains that he was a legend and a hero in Chinese Culture and made a huge impact on society and social studies.

Laozi is traditionally regarded as the author of the "Tao Te Ching" ("Dao-de-jing") 'The Way of Nature', even though its authorship has been debated throughout history. The earliest reliable reference (circa 100 BC) to Laozi is found in the Records of the Grand Historian (Shiji) by Chinese historian Sima Qian (ca. 145–86 BC), which combines three stories:

- In the first, Laozi was said to be a contemporary of Confucius (551-479 BC). His surname was Li (李 "plum"), and his personal name was Er (耳 "ear") or Dan (聃 "long ear"). He was an official in the imperial archives, and wrote a book in two parts before departing to the West.
- In the second he was Lao Laizi ("Old Master") was a contemporary of Confucius, who wrote a book in 15 parts.
- In the third, Laozi was the Grand Historian and astrologer Lao Dan ("Old Long-ears"), who lived during the reign (384-362 BC) of Duke Xian of Qin.

According to popular traditional biographies, he worked as the Keeper of the Archives for the Royal Court of Zhou. This reportedly allowed him broad access to the works of the Yellow Emperor and other classics of the time. The stories assert that Laozi never opened a formal school to teach in, but he nonetheless attracted a large number of students and loyal disciples.

There are numerous variations of a story depicting Confucius consulting Laozi about rituals. In one story[5], Confucius, himself a famous philosopher, consulted Laozi about teaching. He asked, "I have read the Six Classics and consider myself an expert. Yet none of the seventy-two rulers whom I advise have ever put the ideas into practice! What am I doing wrong?"

Laozi answered, "You may have read the Six Classics, but keep in mind that these are only footprints, not the shoes themselves. Look at nature. Each animal reproduces according to its nature. Some are live bearers, some lay eggs, to give you an example. Every species has its own nature and that nature can not be altered! The Tao can not be stopped. When you have the Tao there is not anything you can not do, but if you do not have it, you can not do anything!"

Confucius spent three months, alone in his house, meditating on Laozi's words. When he returned to visit the Master, he said, "I have it now! I understand that each animal reproduces in its own unique way and in accordance with its own nature,. I have my own part in harmony. When I did not teach the rulers in harmony with the natural way, how could I expect to change them?"

Laozi replied, "Now you have got it!". Thus Laozi helped Confucius to guide his actions by the hidden essence, not by external knowledge.

☼ What do you think this 'hidden essence' is, and what does it mean that 'each animal has its own nature and can not be changed'?

(Teachers Note: Although we are all human, we have different natures, can we change? Can we be shown how to do something by someone who is not in tune with us? Should our natural inner-character be nurtured or should we strive to become something that we are not?)

_____

5 Paraphrased from Chuang-tzu, Chapter 15, Legge, 1962

Laozi Leaves China

Traditional accounts state that Laozi grew weary of the moral decay of city life and noted the kingdom's decline. According to these legends, he ventured west to live as a hermit in the unsettled frontier at the age of 160. At the Western gate of the kingdom, he was recognized by a guard, named Yinxi (Wade Giles; Yin Hsi), who was interested in Taoism and had seen Laozi in a Premonition Dream. The Western Pass gate sentry later saw Laozi approaching and asked the old master to be his guest, rest for a while and also produce a record of his wisdom. Laozi wrote his legendary work on strips of bamboo. This is the legendary origin of the creation of the Daodejing: In some versions of the tale, the sentry is so touched by the work that he leaves with Laozi to never be seen again. Some legends elaborate further that the "Old Master" was the teacher of the Buddha, or even possibly the Buddha himself. There are very close connections between Taoism and Mahayana Buddhism, in which followers seek the wisdom of Siddārtha Gautama, the Lord Buddha, son of a warrior Caste Prince.

Daodejing

Laozi's Tao Te Ching ("Dao-de-jing") is *the* most popular work in Chinese philosophy. Only the Christian Bible has been translated and read more times, though this may be changing in this millennium. As with most other ancient Chinese philosophers, Laozi often explains his ideas by way of paradox, analogy, appropriation of ancient sayings, repetition, symmetry, rhyme, and rhythm: old Chinese language being almost like verse or poetry in scripture from. My favourite version of the Daodejing is written by a famous American Poet, Witter Bynner[6], he translated the scripts with the help of his Chinese friend, Dr. Kiang, Kang-hu[7] – himself a poet – who translated from original Chinese into English.

---

6   Harold Witter Bynner (August 10, 1881 – June 1, 1968 – see Wikipedia, http://en.wikipedia.org/wiki/Witter_Bynner

7   In China the Family Name is said first, just like a school register: e.g. Smith, John.

13

<u>Example: Verse 17 by Witter Bynner.</u>

A leader is best

When people barely know that he exists,

Not so good when people obey and acclaim him,

Worst when they despise him.

'Fail to honour people,

They fail to honour you;'

But of a good leader, who talks little,

When his work is done, his aim fulfilled,

They will all say, 'We did this ourselves.'

The Daodejing, often called simply "The Laozi", after its reputed author, describes the Dao (or Tao) as "the mystical source and ideal of all existence": it is unseen, but not transcendent, immensely powerful yet supremely humble, being the root of all things. According to the Daodejing, humans have no special place within the Dao, being just one of its many ("ten thousand things") manifestations. People have desires and free will (and thus are able to alter their own nature). Many act "unnaturally", upsetting the natural balance of the Dao. The Daodejing intends to lead students to a "return" to their natural state, in harmony with Dao. Language and conventional wisdom are critically assessed. Taoism views them as being inherently biased and artificial, widely using paradoxes to sharpen the point.

☼ Can you think of things which are "unnatural" in your environment, or in your country in general?

☼ Can you find just five things that modern industrial science has invented, that are unnatural (e.g. chemical or manufactured synthetics), yet have helped people?

WU-WEI

Wu wei, literally "non-action" or "not acting", is a central concept of the Tao Te Ching or Daodejing. The concept of Wu Wei is very complex and reflected in the words' multiple meanings, even in literal English translation; it can mean "not doing anything", "not forcing", "not acting", in another sense, "acting spontaneously", and "flowing with the moment." Laozi encouraged a change in approach, or "return to nature", rather than false progress: technology may bring about a false sense of progress: technology may have changed but human behaviour has not; many people are blinded by technological gadgets whilst their world around them crumbles into decay and madness.

Humans, if left unguided by Tao, can be self-destructive and we only have to watch the news on television every day to bear out that fact of life. By studying Tao we can strive to make ourselves better people and live happier, more meaningful lives: as long as we do it with Wu Wei – the author has witnessed this state of "automatic natural rule without ruling" in the days of A.M. Citizen's Band radio (c.1979-1982), thousands of people benefited, there was a free and very well organised emergency network, social gatherings and family events, shared community support and much, much more, all self-ruled by the people without anyone claiming to be "leader". There were no hidden agendas, no political motives and no rebellion, it just did not need the government or big business. It worked as a shining example to how people could get on well together, until the government and BT unwisely stepped in and deliberately destroyed it to gain "control".

☼ A good subject for High School level and above? The answer provided by Laozi is not the rejection of technology, but instead seeking the calm state of Wu Wei, free from desires. Wu Wei means, roughly translated, "like water". Those who understand Buddhism will realise that Siddārtha Gautama was enlightened when sitting under a Ban Yan tree by a stream: legend says that he listened to the clear mountain stream bubbling over the rocks and thought about its journey to sea, serving all as it goes; water is simple, it does not act, yet it is life supporting, it flows naturally and always finds its own level.

☼ How can we seek a calm state of Wu Wei without technology?

☼ Do we really need technology? As a point of interest, Dr. Hua, To, who developed Acupuncture, performed the first heart transplant using only needles made from bamboo and natural substances. This was on twin brothers, who volunteered for the experiment which concluded successfully. This was around 700 years before Christ was born, over 2,700 years ago.

Laozi suggested that to follow Tao we should not strive but stay simple, like water, and take a natural path. Water, though soft, is also strong, the strongest and most enduring force on this planet. He used the term broadly with *simplicity* and *humility* as key virtues to live by, often in contrast to *selfish* action. On a political level, it means avoiding such circumstances as war, harsh laws and heavy taxes.

Laozi (portrayed left) is traditionally regarded as the founder of Daoism, intimately connected with the Daodejing and "primordial" (or "original") Daoism.

The story of Laozi took on strong religious overtones since the Han dynasty. As Daoism took root, Laozi was recognized by some as a god. Belief in the revelation of the Dao from the divine Laozi resulted in the formation of the 'Way of the Celestial Master', the first organized religious Daoist sect. In later mature Daoist tradition, Laozi came to be seen as a personification of Dao. He is said to have undergone numerous "transformations", or taken on various guises in various incarnations throughout history to initiate the faithful in the Way. This is how various people translate the same thing, some perhaps being nearer the truth than others. It seems that Laozi was a very observant man and that he had indeed a fine understanding of Tao, but others did not take the time to understand this and maybe that was the reason he gave up "public life" and left the country?

☼ What is Taoism, a religion, a science, simple philosophy, all?

☼ What is "religion"? (Dictionary: 1. the belief in and worship of a god or gods, or 2. a particular system of faith and worship.)

☼ The main religions on planet earth are Christianity, Buddhism, Islam, Atheism, Judaism and Sikhism, to name but a few (for more information go to http://www.bbc.co.uk/religion/religions/). Contemplate whether Christ was a Christian, Buddha was a Buddhist or Muhammad was a Mohammedan? What were they, religious leaders or philosophers or outstanding and enlightened men?

(Teacher's Notes: Religious Terrorism or Education?
Should children be taught religion, especially just one belief? Or should they be enlightened as to the core beliefs of each system or philosophy so that they can note for themselves the similarities and differences. Should children be forced to study one faith, maybe *skimming* partially through other faiths (forcing = terrorism or coercion; terrorism tries to force belief or acceptance by fear or elimination of choice). Many religions were created by followers of one man's ideals and philosophy and share many common principles: except those which have been rewritten for purposes of power and control over the centuries!))

Tao and Creation

The theory behind Tao and the creation of the Universe far pre-dates the modern scientists "Big Bang Theory" by 2,000 years. Taoist teachings, usually handed down by word of mouth, uses simple imagery over the centuries to tell the story like this.

In the beginning there was space, usually seen as a void. There was no life, no action and no planets or stars. We may accept that there was some kind of "matter" in space, gases or elements which formed the basis for the Big Bang" as well as all things that followed. To simplify things Taoism uses the basics, thus starting with an empty void which is meant to represent the Universe before known existence. This emptiness was given the name of Wu Chi ("Wu-ji").

Wu Chi is represented by a black or empty space within a circle. The circle, or ring around it, is symbolic of the Universe. This image and idea is used at the beginning of the practice of Taijiquan, the practitioner emptying their mind and becoming still; this has a great calming effect and clears the mind for practice as well as having beneficial psychological effects, like remaining calm in the face of adversity, if practised regularly enough. Sometimes it is depicted as a white circle with a black edge.

Chaos is sometimes associated with the state of the universe before Wu Chi, as chaos denotes disorganised arrays of many elements which had no purpose, function or interaction.

From Wu Chi sprang life and creation. The Universe erupted into life and created planets, and all other things that we know. This was achieved out of emptiness (described as Yin), by another force Yang (action).

Creation 'Jing'. The two forces spiralling out from the centre of the Universe represent Yin (black) and Yang (white) as they separate and become distinct identities and the Universe as we know it was created (Big Bang). These are the forces behind all things. This is a simple explanation and even peasants who could not read or write at the time could understand these images or ideograms. There are many thousands of things which are either Yin, Yang or a mixture of the two forces. As an example below are just a few easily remembered ones.

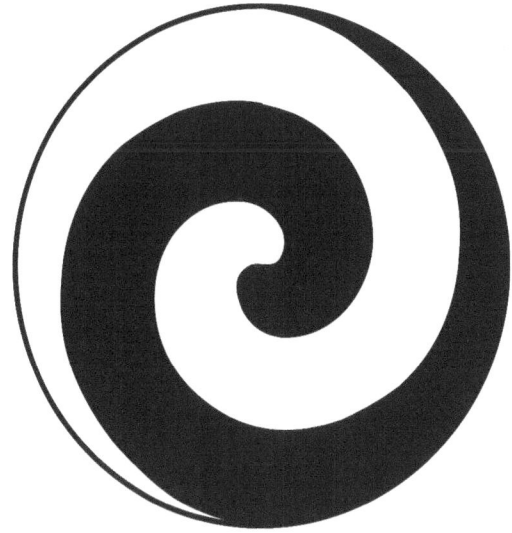

The forces of Tao Yin and Yang, The Eight Directions (Pa Kua or Bagua) and the Five Elements (Wu Hsing or Wuxing), in turn planets were created, stars, solar systems and of course from these sprang all manner of life. Patterns emerged, like day and night, summer and winter, male and female. The Pa Kua, seen here, is often used to decorate Taoist halls, or courtyard areas. It is more than decoration though as students of the way use this to contemplate different meanings and aspects of Tao – and therefore life. The Pa Kua is often used in exercises, like Taoist T'ai Chi Ch'uan, Pa Kua Ch'uan and Hsing-I, alongside the Five Elements and Yin and Yang. They are contemplated and eventually trigger a realisation or action which signifies to the practitioner another step on their journey to enlightenment. Just as we study language, then mathematics and other subjects at school, Taoism is, what I call, a "Lay Science" and doubles as an "Educational Programme" which goes far beyond the basics and enters psychology, sociology and the spiritual realms of life too.

Yin and Yang (Tao)

Taoists used this simple symbol (below) that most people simply call Yin-and-Yang, it is 'Tao'.

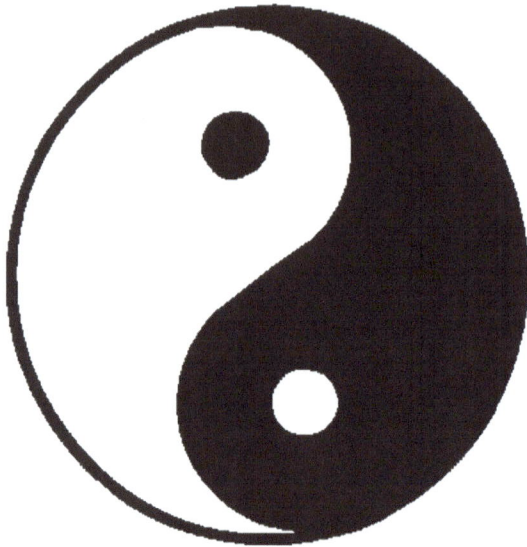

This image represents the constant flow of Yin forces and Yang forces, flowing throughout all things in the Universe. The symbol here depicts 'Harmony', for the two principles work together, like day and night, summer and winter, male and female, and rely on each other for 'Balance', neither one could exist in creation without the other. The "tear-drop" or "fish" shaped sections represent Yin (black) and Yang (white). Neither is superior, yet each may be more prominent at times. They are opposite qualities in phenomena, or principles: e.g. winter is Yin, but gives way to summer which is Yang, this in turn gives way to winter again and so the two work in harmony. If we use the term "forces" it is in the sense of the natural forces of the Universe. Yin and Yang both have the element of the other within them, signifying that neither is 100% pure but also that each needs the other at its core as without Yang Yin could not exist and vice-versa.

Yin: Empty, night, upward or returning qi from earth, cold, dark, female principle, quiet, absorbing, moon, yield, light (weight), passive, nurturing, soft and following.

Yang: Full, day, downward qi from heaven, hot, light, male principle, loud, repelling, sun, push, heavy, aggressive, creating/initiating, hard and leading.

☼ Why not see how many more opposites that you can think of?

20

The Five Elements

or Wu Hsing ("Wu-xing").
The Five Elements are:

- Fire
- Earth
- Metal
- Water
- Wood.

They are noted here in their "creative cycle" - fire induces earth, earth induces metal, metal induces water, water induces wood and wood fire. The creative cycle follows the outer circle in a clockwise direction.

In their "destructive cycle", flowing from point-to-point, fire controls metal, metal controls wood, wood controls earth, earth controls water and water controls fire. The controlling or "destructive" cycle follows from Fire, diagonally down to Metal – at the 5 o'clock position – then continues to Wood, Earth, across to Water and back to Fire. This "relationship" is used in Chinese Astrology and Chinese Medicine, such as Acupuncture: the "Elements" are symbolic of the effects that one diseased organ or function can have on another.

The Eight Directions or Pa Kua, are also symbols of family, actions or function, such as South (Chien) = Heaven, Sun, 'Peng' control. It represents the force of Heaven creating order by control.

Kun, seen here, represents North (Kun) = Earth, 'Lui' receive. It represents the ability to receive and regenerate the creative energy. Solid lines represent Yang, whilst "broken" lines represent Yin. These lines can be mixed in a one-off pattern and each have a representation of functions, etcetera. These symbols are called Trigrams and are made up of three lines each and comprise a set of 8 x 8 = 64 in total. There is no need to go into detail here, especially as this is a compact book that is meant to give an introduction and overview.

Trigrams can be paired to form a Hexagram (six lines). On the right we see a combination of Chien on top and Kun below, this is called P'i and translates as "Stagnation". The Yang is above the Yin, thus controlling it. This creates a situation where the two forces are at an impasse, stagnant. Nothing productive can be achieved. If Kun was on top, this would form T'ai "Prospering", bringing peace as Yin is dominant (see below).

Chinese Horoscopes
In Astrology terms, this analogy my be used to describe the effect a Water Person (born in a Water Element year) may have of "putting out the fire" of a Fire person; e.g. being negative about their passion or ideas. From Chinese Astrology we learn that each person has a particular character, according to their Animal Sign and main Element, but this is then "customised", you might say, by other characteristics such as sub-elements: e.g. Person Born in the year of 1949 in America -

- Year 1949 (Earth)
- Ox (Water)
- Hour of the Snake (Fire)
- Month of Dragon (Wood)
- Country USA (Wood)

These 'elements' will lend themselves to forming character and skills. There will also be Yin or Yang aspects attached to the "birth chart", which may make the person either more or less outgoing, passive or aggressive, etcetera.

☼ I thought you would be curious! Get on the Internet and type into the search bar "books, theodora lau", this should get you 'The Handbook of Chinese Horoscopes (revised), by Theodora Lau. It is very accurate!

The Five Elements and their Yin or Yang variants then give way to "The Ten Thousand Things" - many hundreds of years ago 10,000 was a very big number, but we could equally say Ten Billion Things if we wanted to: it was just making a point that the Five Elements were part of "all things: known and unknown".

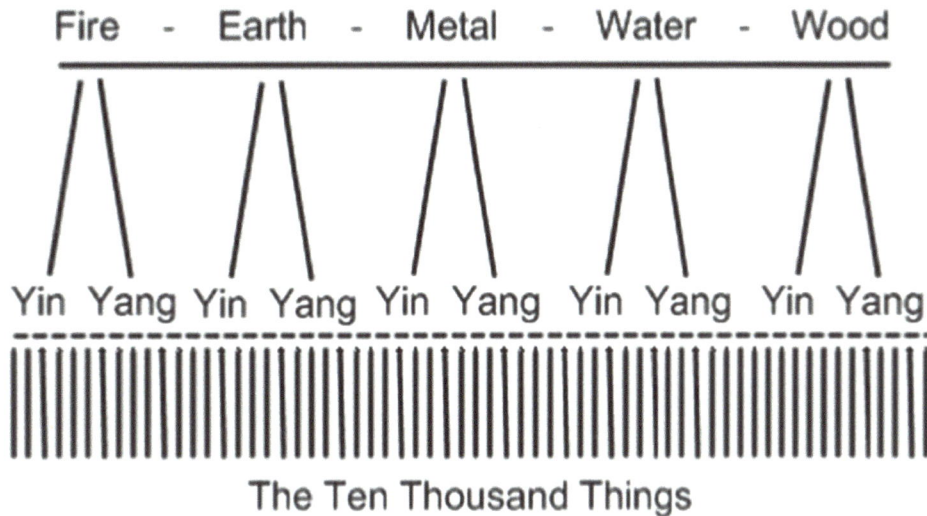

```
Fire  -  Earth  -  Metal  -  Water  -  Wood
_____
  /\      /\       /\        /\        /\
 /  \    /  \     /  \      /  \      /  \
/    \  /    \   /    \    /    \    /    \
Yin Yang Yin Yang Yin Yang Yin Yang Yin Yang
- - - - - - - - - - - - - - - - - - - - - -
||||||||||||||||||||||||||||||||||||||||||||
||||||||||||||||||||||||||||||||||||||||||||
||||||||||||||||||||||||||||||||||||||||||||
         The Ten Thousand Things
```

Take a few simple examples from this we can say that using Wood, a growing tree or plant is Yang, because it is "active", "growing" and "expanding", whereas a wooden Desk is Yin because it is "inactive", "static" and "supportive". In Metal, take a dinner knife; this Yang because it has a sharp blade for cutting. Most tools made out of metal have a yang function, like Pliers, but a Hammer is Yin because it does not have working parts but is wielded by the user who supplies the Yang.

☼ See how many things you can discover the Yin and Yang values of.

Yin	Yang
(Metal) Coin	Moving tool
Railway Track	Locomotive
Car Body	Car Engine
(Wood) Book	Spear
Table	Tree
(Fire) Radiating heat	Flames
Moon	Sun
(Water) Puddle	Rain
Lake	Waterfall
(Earth) concrete floor	Volcano
Soft Clay	Hard Brick

☼ Explore! Some things are only useful for their absence, like a wall, if it did not have spaces in it for doors and windows then how could we use it as a house or school?

The use of these descriptions is purely academic and is not used very much, but it does serve to get someone thinking about *relationships* in all things, therefore having a positive mental/ psychological growth effect as well as helping thought processes along a "guided path", therefore encouraging logic and contemplation, amongst other positive things. It is possible that these images were first produced to illustrate aspects of Tao visually, therefore overcoming language barriers or the inability to read. As far as graphic images are concerned, these are truly great representation of simplicity and effectiveness.

This simple image was used by Taoist Arts Teacher, Professor C. Chee Soo, to illustrate a reply to the question, "How were the two sexes created differently?". He explained, "Tao issues energy from the centre of the Universe[8]. On its outward journey it hit planet Earth and created a downward force in some creatures, pulling the sexual genitals outwards and downwards (male). The energy hits the spinning planet and is returned, on its outward journey it passes through other creatures and created inward genitalia (female). This is the simple theory of how Tao creates male and female."

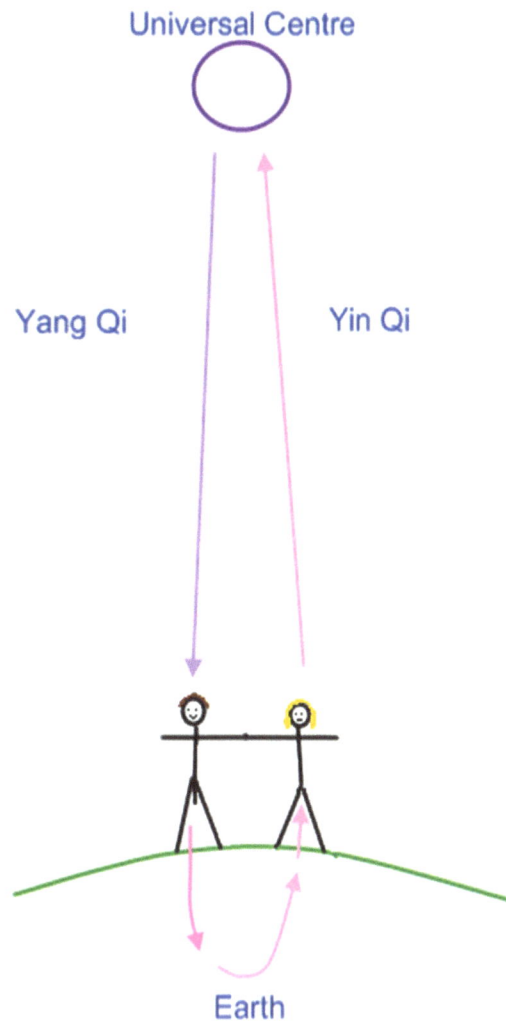

Universal Centre

Yang Qi   Yin Qi

Earth

There is a really delightful simplicity to this theory, but at the same time it lacks detail of *why* some creatures may be influenced by the male principle (Yang) and others by the female principle Yin. The Taoist concept states that "man has his head in the heavens", because of this Ch'i effect, and may explain men's natural inclinations for exploration and discovery. The returning Ch'i passes through women feet first, so giving rise to the expression that "women have their feet on the ground", giving them more earthly properties.

As a general rule of thumb this may be seen in all societies around the globe and even in the animal kingdoms. If contemplated it certainly gives the thought processes a good work-out and may even resolve some of the age old sexist arguments, settling these "wars" between

8   Over two-thousand years ago Tao Scientists agreed that the source of energy issued from a point beyond the Pole Star 'Polaris'. Modern Astrophysicists have pinpointed this as the source of the Big Bang site too.

women and men by having to accept that "men are men and women are women", never shall they be the same, think the same or act the same, no matter how anyone may try to emulate the other. Each, like Yin and Yang in the symbol of Tao, has their own place and their own role in living. Each *should* support the other. If intellect and personal desire are allowed to get in the way (contents of the Psyche left in the "unconscious" which may project in negative ways) then trouble ensues and harmony is disrupted: it is simple to see how pointless sexual wars are, as if neither sex existed then the world would have no human population at all.

Men and Women need to be educated in the ways of harmony, for each has valuable input into life and each has the power to reach inside themselves and understand the "dark side" in order to reveal the "light side" and make life better for all. Self-control leads to regulation and harmony. The Hexagram used here is T'ai (Harmony). T'ai is also the first word in T'ai Chi, meaning, in context to Taoism, "Supreme Ultimate" and is otherwise known as "Tao" (T'ai Chi *Ch'uan* is the Taoist Boxing Exercise, *T'ai Chi* is what it is principled upon). If we combine meanings with the image then it can be used to show us how harmony may be achieved and all people can gain a far better life

Morals.

Generally Taoism shares moral beliefs with many other philosophies, religions and faiths, especially Confucian (and Buddhist which is part originally developed from Taoism, especially Zen in its modern form). Any educated person knows that having better standards of living, sharing space with others, leads to a better life all round. If one resists human temptations and the desire for personal gain by using others in a negative way then this will help improve not only your life but the quality of the world in general: do not feign affection, judge others hastily, use or abuse anyone for personal gain, do not tell lies, make false statements or false allegations or be destructive. These are all symptoms of an unbalanced mind. Help others, try to understand, help where possible without thought of reward. Try to avoid all things false and distracting; including mind-bending drugs and over-involvement in gaming which distracts one from living and practical skills and can undermine subtly. These things all destroy life and damage society.

☼ Students or even groups of friends can discuss the way that one person's actions affect another, and the potential far reaching consequences. This may lead to suppressed emotions or hurt feelings that have not been "dealt with" to come to the surface, if this is the case, get the affected person to make a private note book of their thoughts and feelings so that they can work through their pain and gradually come to understand it better.

This is but one small example of the wisdom of Tao. Protecting Nature is favoured, but not by laws or injunction, simply by being at one with Nature. Taoism encourages students to "look inside" and meditate, thus becoming aware of the deeper sub-conscious: the part that if left to it's own devices can cause trouble; the "unconscious" and "primitive"; this can be exaggerated and "brought out" by incorrect diet and negative living conditions. By knowing what we are capable of we can take time, meditate on the for and against elements and make educated decisions based upon the "conscious" and enlightened mind. This is progress and change; change is the only constant in life, positive change is growth, negative change is decay.

Bullying.
As this book is used in schools, it is worth mentioning here the psychology of bullying. Someone who is acting like a bully usually has problems at home: these can range from abuse, such as violence or sexual, it can be fears about family health or poverty, someone is bullying them that fear so they then think it is fair to bully others. This is another issue that can be dealt with by sitting down and talking, saying that you want to understand their problems and be their friend. Humans are "pack animals", like wolves, so fair better when the pack is supportive.

☼ Any discussion of the above should not be controlled but simply monitored for the intrusion of personal grief or an opinion formed through grief. Logic, philosophy and common sense should be allowed to prevail, keeping the subject on Yin and Yang, harmony and working together: if the subject turns to sex, as in "men have sex and women have babies", then the teacher should gently guide students away by informing them that this is just a natural principle and not the entire essence of one's life; sex or sexuality is not what life is made of, merely a talking point of those who have no wider view of life, in which sex, procreation and motherly or fatherly roles play just a small part; "life" and the far broader "quality of life" *is* the essence.

Tao and Living Today.

Although seated in the distant past and founded in principle over 5,000 years ago, Taoism is just as relevant today as it has ever been. In fact, probably more so. Young people have developed a critical manner towards the main religions and an attitude of disbelief and much disappointment. To appreciate Tao though a person must study Tao for a long time: it takes a long time to study any subject, but the Way of Life, The Universe and "everything" can only take years! However, this is not a daunting task, it is pleasurable as one sees many benefits from enlightenment along the path.

Taoist philosophy helps us to understand life better and be more free from worry or dwelling on a one-sided action. By informing us that reality and illusion, good and bad, pure and impure, nice and nasty all exist side by side, that they are all part of life's natural cycles and events, we can begin to accept what happens. This does not make it "right" however, as right and wrong are again just descriptions we use to help us learn and understand.

Using these simplistic descriptions we can take a very common example, a person who does something that hurts us. If you look at this situation from both a Taoist and Psychology point of view, the person who does the wrong is "sick" and like Influenza in a physical sense, this sickness is then passed on to another unwilling victim. This is the nature of underdeveloped humans who let their "dark side" unwittingly release negative acts upon the world and its inhabitants. It is not the victim's fault and they should try to accept this fact. The term "sick" should not really be used, nor should "normal" when applied to someone who places themselves as being "not sick" - normality covers all things in life, but it is used to distinguish instead: a person in a "normal" state does nothing to hurt a fellow human, whereas someone who is in a "sick" state does something socially unacceptable: this is how humans view, consider and then categorise, so that they can distinguish between actions and may be said to be "normal" in terms of human behaviour.

According to Taoism, a "cultivated" person is far less likely to cause harm to another and will also survive attacks better than those who are not prepared. A cultivated person is taken as someone who has studied 'The Way' and who may understand most aspects of living, including being able to let emotions and feelings come and go naturally without hanging on to them. Sometimes this type of person is called a Sage or "enlightened". The enlightened Sage can be in a voluntary position to help others who are struggling to understand, or are in trouble. These aspects are also part of Wu Wei, to flow or live naturally and without conscious effort: accept all things and lead by example, not force, for a person who uses force is disliked, whereas a person who lives a non-interfering life is admired.

Consciousness and Unconsciousness.
Jung called these the "twin states of being" in human behaviour. He said that when the contents of the Psyche were left in the unconscious, they may be projected in a negative way, outwards into the world of matter. Most people just accept these negative events and label them as "fate". He goes on to say that if the contents were made conscious, then the person concerned would realise inner truth. This follows the concepts of Taoism as a person who studies Tao studies themselves, their inner state, then the state of the world around them and gradually expands their consciousness. When they reach this stage they become, what most people would describe as, enlightened. Then those people do not let their undiscovered unconscious reign havoc, instead choosing a better path, one which is Wu Wei. However, helping others is also a concept of the enlightened, so involvements in "life skills" like natural medicine, natural exercise, healing and diet, education by transmitting information and offering help where genuinely needed

and wanted are all associated with Taoism. Taoism has some very practical things to offer culture.

Laozi, in the Daodejing, observed many things in life and wrote in the essence: Verse 52.(Translated by Witter Bynner & Dr. Kiang)

The source of life
Is as a mother.
Be fond of both mother and children but know the mother dearer
And you outlive death.
Curb your tongue and senses
And you are beyond trouble,
Let them loose
And you are beyond help.
Discover that nothing is too small for clear vision,
Too insignificant for tender strength,
Use outlook
And insight,
Use them both
And you are immune:
For you have witnessed eternity.

☼ This verse can be discussed and a group of individuals could write it down, take it away and study it, then come back and discuss personal ideas they have gained from it.

Laozi suggests here that we should avoid human error by curbing our tongues, and respect the Universal Powers and creation as we would our family with our cherished mother at the head: the one who gives us life and nurtures us from birth to adulthood. Nothing is too small to think about, or too insignificant for giving our love or time to. Use a positive mindset with penetrative thinking, but keep your minds open, and you will be immune to the perils of life (not immune from being targeted, but less vulnerable and better prepared). To "witness eternity" is a parallel which suggests loosely that by adopting this thoughtful and inquisitive approach whilst harmonising with Tao, you will come to understand life and the Universe – as opposed to feeling isolated or disjointed and not understanding what is happening to you or around you.

Taoism and Leadership.

Political theorists influenced by Laozi have advocated humility in leadership and a restrained approach to statecraft, for either ethical reasons, pacifist reasons, or even for tactical ends. In a different context, various anti-authoritarian movements have embraced the Laozi teachings on the power of the weak. Below is another translated verse from the Daodejing.

"Knowing others is intelligence;
    knowing yourself is true wisdom.
    Mastering others is strength;
        mastering yourself is true power."

This is the basic history and influence of the two great fathers of Taoism, Huang-di and Laozi. Although they spent much time in thought and wrote down their findings, which became a legacy of immeasurable value, they advocated not reading books, or blindly following or worshipping others, or idols, but finding out for yourself the truth about life and the great Tao.

"A journey of a thousand [miles] starts with a single step."

Chuang-tzu was a prominent philosopher. The one thing that most people remember him for was his interpretation of a dream: one night he had a dream that he was a Butterfly, flitting about from flower to flower in a meadow. The dream was so clear that when he awoke he wondered, "Am I a man asleep dreaming that I am a Butterfly, or a Butterfly dreaming that I am a man waking up?" This reflects the Taoist acceptance of Yin and Yang, opposites, in this case illusion and Reality.

Many people have dreams, but which is real and which is illusion? Sometimes we have dreams that are very real and feel as though we are there, experiencing thoughts, feelings and emotions, even touch sensations. There is an old saying in Taoism, "Believe nothing you hear and only 50% of what you see." However you believe things to be, life should be studied carefully and not taken for granted. It is is sadly a condition of human nature that in a contrived society (modern cultures, governments and power-mongers) that people weave complicated and destructive webs of deception as a means to their own ends. Young people should not fall into this trap as it does not create happiness but anger and mistrust. Be yourself, do not feign affection or contrive to make things happen. In Taoism the word "natural" applies to all things. Chuang-tzu was a great supporter of letting the natural character come out of people, and that this will lead to good. If a character is forced, suppressed or "moulded" it will lead to unhappiness.

Note: By naming one thing good we make another thing bad. This is "convention" purely for illustration. See 'Feelings and Emotions'.

Taoist Arts.

These include T'ai Chi Ch'uan, Ch'i Kung, Feng Shui (natural arrangement), Traditional Chinese Medicine (TCM) and Acupuncture, organic farming, herbs, foods and dietary balance, Five Element cooking, cosmology, exercise for illness prevention or correction, scientific numeracy and much more.

Taoism has also lead to many Chinese inventions, like gunpowder and rocketry, the magnetic compass, irrigation and crop planting, seafaring, typewriters and computers, porcelain, special metal alloys and even optical eye-glasses (as presented to Marco Polo when he was visiting and discovering China), plus much more that modern society perhaps takes for granted.

The Taoist Arts are practised by anyone on two levels, usually. The first is as a recommended course of exercise for general health and fitness improvements; sometimes this may be recommended by a Doctor, as many Chinese Doctors tell their patients to take up T'ai Chi

Ch'uan or Ch'i Kung, for specific diseases (dis-ease) or weaknesses.Secondly they are practised on a wider or more serious scale by Taoists (people who study Tao) as a partial method of getting their body naturally healthy and "in tune" with Tao's natural harmonics; these often combine with long periods of meditations and study of Taoist texts.

(*Picture: A technique from Taijiquan known as Single Whip - performed her by the author.*)

Unlike other, more common practises that we call Martial Arts, yoga type exercises, etcetera, the Taoist Arts are all developed within the framework, the philosophy, of TAO, or Nature's Way. The objective of these practices is to slowly de clutter the body and mind and become more in harmony with Tao (The Universal Way), thus avoiding many problems, illnesses, mental health issues and more.

We are Human animals, but if we look at other animals, in their natural environment, they do not suffer from the unnatural illnesses or anxieties that the "tamed" Human Animal does: and more so in larger towns and cities. You can see how captivity affects them in Zoos though, where wild cats can be seen pacing up and down: a sign of anxiety.

Summary.

Taoism, especially after Dr. Carl Jung's interest and involvements, has become widely used in psychology and psychiatry. It can do more.

Taoism can be used in education, as it already is in health, science, medical (TCM) and other aspects of life.

Many studies by people involved in these pursuits end up "full circle", so to speak, coming back to study Tao and Taoism. It is not possible to reinvent the wheel, but the wheel may be used for other applications.

T'ai Chi Ch'uan or Taijiquan has also drawn much interest, at first just for its relaxing benefits, later for its deeper and more meaningful philosophical approach which directly connects to lifestyle and life's decisions. In 1980's I predicted recorded my thoughts on East and West, saying that the Industrial Revolution is now spreading to China, and they would be the great manufacturers and producers, while in the West we take a break. Thus leaving us with more leisure time (another Yin to Yang and Yang to Yin flow), and that here in the west, in the future, we would be seeking more enlightenment, this would come from the East – another Yin-Yang action, like day and night.

My prediction has now come true:
many Chinese have been forced to forget traditional ways and beliefs and are now seeking "industrial fulfilment", whilst here in the West we are seeking better ways and looking to older eastern beliefs; ironically, many "new" Chinese are also seeking their old ways, but are having to move to achieve this.

This cycle is part of the spiral, progress and change.

Such is The Way.

The Power In Not Contending.

To posses the Power (Tao) that runs deep
Is to be like a newborn child.

Poisonous insects do not sting it,
Fierce beasts do not seize it,
Birds of prey do not strike it.

Its bones are yielding,
its muscles relaxed,
Its grip is strong.

It does not know yet the union of male and female,
Yet its virility is active.
Its Life Force is at its greatest.
It can scream all day,
Yet it does not become hoarse.
Its harmony is at its greatest.

To know harmony is called the Absolute.
To know the Absolute is called Insight.
To enhance life is called propitious (lucky or favourable).
To be conscious of Influence is called strength.

Things overgrown must decline.
This is not the Tao.
What is not the Tao will soon end.

Translation of Verse 55 by
R. L. Wing. (Book), The Tao
of Power'.

The Mysterious 'Unwritten Verse'.

The Spirit of TAO

In 1995 the author was compelled, by some unseen energy, to stop work, switch on his computer and Word Processor software. Sitting puzzled for a few seconds, looking at a blank page and thinking "What am I doing this for?". Fingers reached for the keyboard and started typing the following verse, including the title, the words flowed to paper without pause and without thought, "like dictation, but without the voice!". It remains in tact and unedited, as is. There was surprise when I read it afterwards. Such has been my life, a "tool" of the Way.

> The TAO has no name, no form.
> No words can describe it, so vast is The Way,
> So immense The Universe.
>
> From inaction comes action.
> The Tao is action.
> Action has no fixed form.
> Form has creation.
> Creation has meaning.
>
> The Way is my tool.
> I am a tool of The Way.
> Where Tao cannot be heard,
> Then I am its voice.
> Where Tao cannot be seen,
> I can paint an image.
> Where Tao cannot be touched,
> I can touch and be touched.
>
> Where words fall upon the ears.
> And then fade away,
> Ink flows to paper,
> And words stay.
>
> Tao is there for everyone.
> Tao has much to say!

'Lao Tzu's Unwritten Verse'
of the Tao Te Ching
Recorded by Myke Symonds©, February 1995.

Personal Notes:

Bibliography.

Ch'ang Ming – Long Life Diet.
By C. Chee Soo. - (Seahorse Arts Press)

Tai Chi Diet: food for life / Tai Chi Diet: Chang Ming.
By Professor Myke Symonds. - Life Force publishing.

The Tao of Power. (A new translation of the Tao Te Ching)
By R. L. Wing. - The Aquarian Press.

The I Ching Workbook.
By R. L. Wing. - The Aquarian Press.

Qigong and Baduanjin.
By Professor Myke Symonds. - Life Force publishing.

The Handbook of Chinese Horoscopes.
By Theodora Lau. - Harper Collins.

T'ai Chi Ch'uan and The Code of Life.
Graham Horwood. - Singing Dragon press.
(Note: I've only just started reading this, but it has already reminded me of past studies and enlarged information previously gathered. Very good.)

The Way of Life – according to Laozu.
Wytter Bynner. - in Reprint (search Amazon).

Wikipedia.
Public "open source" Information and Reference tool.

End Note: The author has spent 48 years teaching (to 2021) and many more in study and practice. He enjoys imparting knowledge and helping individuals or the community gain skills for a better life and is deeply indebted to all who have made Tao their life's work an have passed on their knowledge.

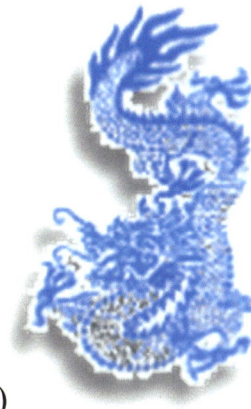

www.ingramcontent.com/pod-product-compliance
Lightning Source LLC
Chambersburg PA
CBHW041427090426
42741CB00002B/63